WITNESS TO WAR

WORLD WAR I

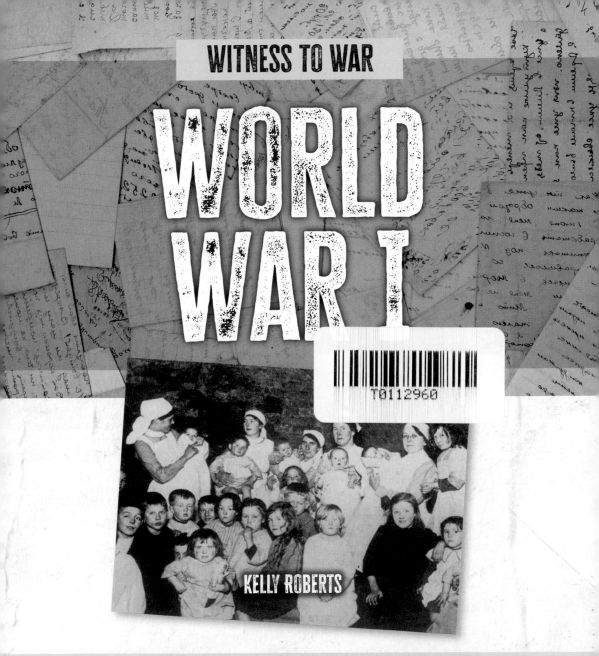

KELLY ROBERTS

What can we learn from the people who witnessed war?

CHERITON
CHILDREN'S BOOKS

Published in 2025 by **Cheriton Children's Books**
1 Bank Drive West, Shrewsbury, Shropshire, SY3 9DJ, UK

Copyright 2025 Cheriton Children's Books

First Edition

Author: Kelly Roberts
Designer: Paul Myerscough
Editor: Sarah Eason
Proofreader: Katie Dicker

Printed in China

Please visit our website,
www.cheritonchildrensbooks.com
to see more of our high-quality books.

CONTENTS

CHAPTER 1

WORLD WAR I

In the summer of 1914, Europe was plunged into a devastating war that would claim millions of lives and last for more than four years. This conflict, which people at the time called the Great War, did not just change the lives of the millions of men who fought in it. It also had a huge impact on families and children who were often far from the front line. They would witness the devastation of war—and in doing so, become a witness to history. In this book we will look at some of their stories and their words as witnesses to war.

The Path to War

For a century before 1914, the nations of Europe had lived mostly in peace with each other, but rivalries and jealousies had built up. Prussia and many smaller states had united to form the mighty German Empire. Germany was a rival, not only to her neighbor France but also to the British Empire. Russia and Austria-Hungary were competing for power in Eastern Europe, but smaller countries, such as Serbia and Bosnia-Herzegovina, wanted to rule themselves.

WITNESSES TO WAR

In this book we will hear the words of witnesses to the war: the people who experienced the conflict firsthand. We'll discover what impact the war had on them and what we can learn from their accounts. In each case, read the source and the notes, then try to answer the questions.

Millions of soldiers, like the ones shown here, were injured or lost their lives in the war.

A Shot Is Fired

When Archduke Franz Ferdinand, heir to the throne of Austria-Hungary, was shot by Serbian **nationalists** on June 28, 1914, the complex system of alliances and rivalries meant that, within a few weeks, most of Europe was at war.

War on a World Stage

World War I was fought between Germany and Austria-Hungary on one side, and the combined armies of Great Britain, France, Russia, and their allies on the other side. As the conflict went on, other countries were dragged into it. Fighting spread to Asia and Africa. In 1917, the United States finally joined the war on the side of Great Britain, France, and their allies. It was now truly a world war.

The **assassination** of Archduke Franz Ferdinand was a turning point in the lead-up to the war.

Lives Forever Changed

During World War I, people's lives changed beyond recognition. Men left their families behind to prepare for battle, and women began working in jobs formerly carried out by men. This meant that many people were separated from their families for a long time, and their lives were forever changed.

The Front Line in Focus

The war meant that children's fathers were away on the front line and their mothers now worked in jobs away from the home—often in military factories where they helped make **ammunition** for soldiers fighting in the war. With all efforts focused on sending supplies to the front line, certain foods, such as those made from wheat, were less available. Women had to change the way they worked, and the foods they cooked for their families.

A Changed Childhood

Life for children became very different during World War I, compared with how it had been before the war. Children became responsible for many of the jobs that their mothers would previously have done at home. There was much less time to play because there were now many more daily chores to do.

This image shows a soldier who has returned home to his family for a brief **respite** from the war.

WITNESS TO WAR

This short letter was written by a British soldier named Stephen Brown. He was stationed in France in December 1914, and killed just a few months later, in May 1915.

Dear Mother
Just a line to let you know that I am quite well. I am for the Front on Tuesday. But if you write to the Commanding Officer and say I am only seventeen, it will stop me from going. Get it here before Tuesday for I cannot get a pass to come and see you. Don't forget.
From Stephen

In British law, soldiers had to be 19 to fight overseas in 1914. However, many young men claimed to be older so they could join the war.

How do you think Stephen was feeling when he wrote these words? What effect do you think they may have had on his mother when she read them?

Tough News, Tough Life

Not only did the day-to-day lives of children in wartime families become physically harder, but children became emotionally tougher, too. They had to deal with the threat that their fathers and brothers could be injured or even killed in battle. Families dreaded the arrival of a message by telegram or mail that told them that a father, brother, uncle, cousin, or son on the front line had been injured or killed.

Loved ones said tearful goodbyes to soldiers as they left to fight in the war.

CHAPTER 2

THE FIRST GLOBAL WAR

World War I was not only the first global war—it was also the first major conflict to be fought on land, sea, and in the air. Vast land armies faced each other on the battlefields of Europe. Land troops also fought in the very different terrain of Africa and the Middle East. For the first time, aircraft were used to attack enemy troops and civilians.

Mapping the War

The main battle zones were the **Western** and **Eastern Fronts** in Europe. After Germany's initial invasion of Belgium and northern France, the Western Front hardly moved until 1918. It was made up of hundreds of miles of trenches, stretching from France's border with Switzerland up to the North Sea. The Eastern Front was longer and more changeable, as Russians, Germans, and Austrians battled across the lands of Eastern Europe.

PRIMARY SOURCE

Fighting in a Strange Land

This 1886 map shows the British Empire, which included all the countries shaded in blue, such as Australia, Canada, and India. Though far from Europe, these countries sent soldiers to fight for Britain. How do you think it must have felt for the men sent to battle to be fighting so far from home? Many of them would not have experienced travel to another country and different cultures before the war.

Kaiser Wilhelm II (on the left) is shown here inspecting German soldiers who were fighting in the war. Wilhem II was the Emperor of Germany until the end of the war.

The War on the Waves

Control of the sea routes to Europe was still vital for both sides, although the Battle of Jutland in 1916 was the only major naval battle of the war. From the beginning of the war, Britain used its navy to prevent food and supplies reaching Germany and Austria-Hungary. This may have helped the Allies win the war, but it also led to terrible food shortages for families in Central Europe, causing hundreds of thousands of deaths from starvation.

Sinking Ships

Germany used submarines—called U-boats—to keep ships from reaching Britain and France. Hundreds of ships were sunk by submarines. Many of them were carrying food and war supplies such as ammunition, but ships also brought troops to Europe from as far away as Australia, New Zealand, and the United States.

The War in the Air

In 1914, aircraft were still just a few years old, but they were soon adapted for use in wartime. Both sides used airplanes to gather information on enemy trenches and troop movements. They were also used to bomb trenches and fight each other in the air. Aircraft technology was still very new, and being a pilot was one of the most dangerous jobs of the war.

War on the Western Front

When war broke out in August 1914, the German army did all it could to win a quick victory against France. In an attempt to do so, the army invaded **neutral** Belgium, but that led to Britain declaring war. After weeks of bloody battles, the German advance was halted at the Battle of the Marne, near Paris. German forces defended their positions by digging trenches that would protect them from enemy **artillery** and machine gun fire.

Brutal Battles

In the years that followed, armies tried heroically to break through the enemy's line of trenches. Hundreds of thousands of men were killed and wounded in terrible confrontations such as the Battle of Verdun and the Battle of the Somme in 1916. Between the battles, soldiers had to deal with constant danger, cold, and boredom. Trenches were infested with rats and lice, and soldiers could instantly be shot by a sniper's bullet if they stuck their head above ground.

PRIMARY SOURCE

Living Underground

There were usually three or more lines of trenches on each enemy's side, connected by communication trenches. Soldiers would spend a few days at a time in the frontline trench, but spent more time in support trenches, living in underground shelters or dugouts. This photograph shows a soldier reading a book. Why do you think distractions such as this or letter writing were so important to soldiers living in trenches during the war?

WITNESS TO WAR

This account was written by Frances Gulick. She worked as a volunteer cafeteria worker close to the Western Front during the war. Here she remembers how she felt when her parents visited her:

" After the first thrill of the meeting, the presence of my parents in Gondrecourt gave me the queerest feeling ... Home was incredibly remote. News of my friends with whom I had grown up seemed curiously flat and trivial. They lived in another world, which had ceased to concern me a great deal."

Gondrecourt is in northeastern France, more than 4,800 miles (7,724 km) from the United States.

Frances talks about her friends and world back home in the United States as seeming "curiously flat and trivial." Why do you think ordinary life might appear so to her after her experience of witnessing war?

What effect do you think her experience may have had on her mind and her emotions?

Life in the trenches was boring as well as brutal. When not fighting, soldiers occupied themselves as best they could.

The War in Eastern Europe

With neither side making progress on the Western Front, military leaders hoped that Russia's huge army would be able to defeat Germany and Austria-Hungary in the east. The war on the Eastern Front, however, was fought over a much wider area than the war in the West. During the war years, land in Poland and elsewhere was often controlled by one side, then the other. Neither could make a decisive breakthrough when so much of Germany's strength was focused on attacking France and Great Britain in the West.

A Bitter Russian War

Russia could **mobilize** millions of soldiers, but they were often poorly equipped and badly led. As the war developed, some did not even have rifles or warm clothes to cope with the bitter winter weather.

PRIMARY SOURCE

Growing Hunger

The war on the Eastern Front destroyed farms and villages, like this one. It also took many farm laborers away from their families and the land they farmed. Without them, food production collapsed and hunger became a problem for the women and children left behind, as well as for the men on the front line. Many families in land controlled by Austria-Hungary also faced hunger, as a **blockade** by the British and French navies kept food from reaching Central Europe. How may this have affected support for the war, both for the soldiers on the front line and the families they had left behind?

Russian soldiers, like those shown below, were very badly equipped compared to the Germans. As a result, they struggled to gain ground on the Eastern Front.

Starving Soldiers

Millions of troops were taken prisoner on the Eastern Front. They relied on food being sent from home and, when food shortages began to take hold, prisoners of war often did not have enough to eat and starved.

Forced to Flee

Ordinary families suffered as a direct result of fighting on the Eastern Front. When Russian forces retreated across Poland in 1915, many thousands of Polish families were forced to leave their homes and flee from the soldiers.

Suffering in Serbia

One country that suffered more than almost any other was Serbia. Austria-Hungary's attack on Serbia was the first action of the war, but this small country in the Balkans did not give in easily. Serbian resistance held out, although men, women, and children were massacred by the invaders. Serbia was finally invaded by German and Bulgarian armies in December 1915. More than one-quarter of the country's population was killed or wounded in the war.

The War in the Middle East and Africa

Germany, France, and especially Great Britain controlled lands outside the borders of Europe. These **colonies** were soon dragged into the war as British forces, which included Indian and African troops, seized African lands that Germany had controlled. Fighting in the hot, humid rain forests of Africa was very different from the cold and mud of the Western Front. When the **Ottoman Empire** joined the war in October 1914, Turkish lands in the Middle East also saw military campaigns. President Woodrow Wilson was determined that the United States would stay neutral.

Not Our Fight

The campaigns outside Europe were not just fought by European troops or those who had traveled from places such as Australia. Many Africans were forced to join the war, either as support workers or even as troops. These people had to leave their families, but often had little idea what they were fighting for.

Terror in Turkey

In 1915, Allied leaders decided to attack Turkey, believing it was weaker than Germany or Austria-Hungary. They launched a daring attack at Gallipoli in the Dardanelles, a narrow part of the Turkish Straits linking the Mediterranean Sea and Black Sea. The attack was a disaster, and many of those who died were soldiers from Australia and New Zealand, fighting thousands of miles from their families.

These British prisoners of war (POWs) were taken captive by Turkish soldiers. Some are bandaged and sleeping in quarters in a tent. Many more were killed.

WITNESS TO WAR

Irish soldier Henry Hanna took part in the Gallipoli campaign of 1915. This is an extract from his account of the event:

What effect do you think the sights that Henry saw may have had on him after the battle?

"Then came my dash for safety. I made two rushes of it, and had to shout to our fellows to stop firing to allow me to get in. I got a splinter of a bullet in the side. It just pricked the skin and stuck in my belt. There is a hole in my belt where it stuck .... The sights I saw going along that place I shall never forget. Some of our fellows throwing back the bombs which the Turks threw over, and which had not exploded. Wounded and dead lying everywhere. The sun streaming down, and not a drop of water to be had."

The Allies did not believe that the Turkish soldiers, shown below, would be as well equipped as they were. They met surprisingly fierce resistance from the Turks during the attack at Gallipoli.

What do you think it would have been like to fight in this extreme heat, without any water?

CHAPTER 3

WOMEN AND THE WAR

Wororld War I was one of the first wars to create huge armies of **conscripted** soldiers. Millions of men were drafted into the military and forced to leave their homes, jobs, and families. Even the United States drafted millions of men after joining the war in 1917. With their husbands and sons away fighting the war, many of them returning injured or not at all, women's lives changed dramatically.

PRIMARY SOURCE

Women Workers

World War I caused big changes in the world of work, as more women began to fill jobs vacated by men who were fighting at the front line.

Women took on jobs in heavy industry such as shipbuilding and working on railroads, like the women shown in this photograph, which were previously carried out only by men. Homelife also changed as women had to care for their families without the support of husbands and grown-up sons. What effect do you think the new role women played in the workforce had on families?

A Different Life

Before the war broke out, the lives of women across Europe and North America were very different from those of most women today. Very few had the chance to get the education and training necessary for professional jobs such as doctor or engineer. Many women went to work after leaving school in their early teens but would stop working when they got married. There were few labor-saving devices such as refrigerators or washing machines to help women manage housework and their families' needs.

This photograph shows American women weighing wire coils. The wire was used on the battlefield to create barriers to slow down or stop the enemy.

WITNESS TO WAR

This account was written by Ethel Dean, who worked in a British factory, making weapons for soldiers on the front line:

"Everything that powder touches goes yellow. All the girls' faces were yellow, all round their mouths. They had their own canteen, in which everything was yellow that they touched ... Everything they touched went yellow – chairs, tables, everything."

The girls were yellow because of contact with Trinitrotoluene (TNT), which was an explosive used in ammunitions. Women who worked with TNT were often called "canaries" because of the yellow color of their skin. TNT is toxic and turns the skin yellow. Some women died from TNT poisoning if they were in contact with it for a long time.

Why do you think women carried on working in such difficult and dangerous conditions during the war?

Do you think people would be prepared to make similar sacrifices today?

Women in the Workplace

Before the war, many women went to work before they were married. Working-class families often depended on the money both parents could earn in factories. Millions of women also worked as cooks, maids, and domestic servants in the houses of wealthy families.

Women Taking Jobs

Once war broke out, all the warring countries soon started to employ women in jobs that had been vacated by men serving in the military forces. In France, women worked as conductors on the streetcars. In Britain, women were also employed as drivers on London's buses. Before 1914, it had been unusual for women to work in offices in many countries, but this became common and was a lasting change as a result of the war.

Making Weapons

The warring nations had to supply their frontline forces with huge amounts of artillery **shells** and bullets to keep the war going. By the end of the war, **munitions** factories in Britain employed 950,000 women, compared to 700,000 in Germany.

This American woman is welding a water jacket for a machine gun. The water jacket kept the gun from overheating.

PRIMARY SOURCE

We Need You!

In 1917 and 1918, the demand for women workers grew in the United States, as men enlisted to fight in the war. As in Europe, women also began to fill jobs in heavy industry. One newspaper reported that, in just a few months, the number of women working on the Pennsylvania Railroad had more than doubled to nearly 4,000 employees. Women worked in munitions factories, like this one in Connecticut, to build guns and other weapons that were used on the front line. Their contribution would help determine the outcome of the war.

Not Equal

For many women, the war brought new freedoms, and higher-paid jobs than they had before the war. However, although women were taking over men's jobs, they were usually paid less than male workers. **Labor unions** often opposed women taking these jobs and insisted that men would get their jobs back at the end of the war.

Land Labor

The supply of food was as important as the supply of gunpowder in winning the war. From 1914, the British navy tried to keep food and supplies from reaching Germany by sea. German U-boats fought back, sinking ships bound for Britain and France. The warring nations in Europe used as much land as they could to grow food, and women had to replace men working on the land.

Female Farmers

Female members of farming communities had always played their part, particularly when the harvest was gathered. As men volunteered to fight, women and children took on a bigger role in running their farms. Later in the war, as men were drafted to serve in the war, and trade blockades started to have an impact, shortage of labor in farming became a major problem. In Britain, the Women's Land Army (WLA) was launched in March 1917. By the end of the war, around 300,000 women were working on farms.

PRIMARY SOURCE

Women of America

Inspired by the British organization, the Women's Land Army of America (WLAA) was set up by women in the United States. This photograph shows some of the women who were part of the organization. They were also known as farmerettes. By 1919, the WLAA had more than 20,000 members. Many of the WLAA volunteers were college students, with little experience of farmwork. What do you think it must have been like to become a farmerette? What do you think the challenges may have been? Do you think women may have found it a positive experience?

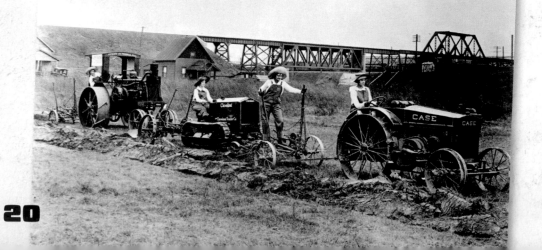

WITNESS TO WAR

Ida Purnell was a member of the WLAA and worked in California. She took her work seriously, as detailed in her account below:

"I made it clear that a slacker was a person who tried to palm off poor boxes of grapes for good ones. One bad bunch ruins a whole box, and that is the same as helping shoot cannonballs at our boys."

Why do you think Ida describes ruining a box of grapes as like shooting cannonballs at US soldiers? What does that tell us about the importance of food during wartime?

Women Workers

Many people were shocked at the news of women working in organizations such as the WLAA. They did not believe that women should work outdoors driving tractors, plowing fields, and wearing trousers! But when one member of the WLAA was challenged about her role and asked whether the women would find the work too hard and return to the cities, she simply replied, "Would we quit? No, soldiers don't!"

These are some of the members of the WLAA. The women posed proudly for their photograph, aware of how important their contribution was to the ongoing war.

Witnessing the Truth

Wounded soldiers were usually treated close to the front line, and many buildings in northern France were converted into field hospitals. More serious injuries would lead to **evacuation** to their home countries. Wounded soldiers were usually transported part of the way in hospital trains, like the one shown in this photograph, and treated by nurses as they traveled. The nurses would have dealt with horrific wounds and terrible injuries.

What impact do you think that may have had on the nurses? How may it have changed their feelings about the war?

Women and the Wounded

It was not just on the land or in the factories making boots, bombs, and bread that women had an impact. Just a few weeks after the start of the war, it was already clear that it would be a long and bloody conflict, and thousands of nurses would be needed to care for the wounded.

A Respectable Job

Nursing was one area of war that women had been involved with before. Mary Seacole had led the way during the Crimean War of the 1850s. Nursing was seen as a more respectable job than working in a factory, and nurses were often young women from wealthier families, who volunteered because they wanted to help the war effort, rather than because they needed to work in order to feed their families.

On the Front Line

Organizations such as the British Voluntary Aid Detachments (VADs) had formed before the outbreak of war. The VADs were open to women and men, but most men volunteered or were drafted into the frontline forces. The VAD members worked as nurses and ambulance drivers close to the front line, where they faced the constant danger of being caught up in the fighting that took place there.

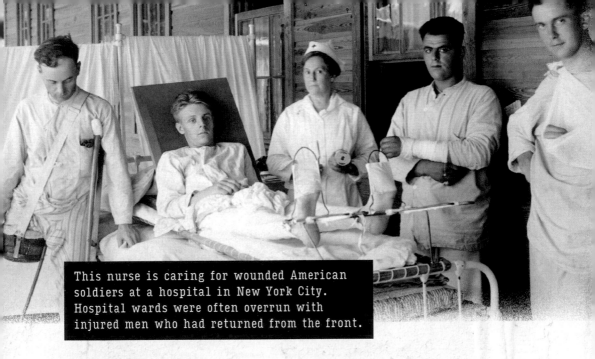

This nurse is caring for wounded American soldiers at a hospital in New York City. Hospital wards were often overrun with injured men who had returned from the front.

Heading Overseas

The National League for Women's Service was the US equivalent of the VADs. The League filled many roles, including supplying trained radio operators. Just a few weeks after the United States joined the war in 1917, trained American nurses were already on their way to Europe. Here, they set up field hospitals to support US troops. By the end of the war, more than 21,000 nurses were enlisted in the US military, and around 10,000 of them were serving overseas.

Nurses had to care for patients who had suffered horrific, life-changing injuries.

Helping the War Effort

Women—working as nurses, on the land, in factories, offices, and elsewhere—played a vital part in the war effort on both sides. They did not usually fight in the trenches but, especially in the later years, women were able to join the military forces in support roles, such as cooking food and driving military vehicles.

Female volunteers, like this Salvation Army worker, wrote letters for injured soldiers to help them keep in touch with their families back home.

PRIMARY SOURCE

Lifting Spirits

This postcard shows female Salvation Army volunteers cooking on the front line in France. They are making doughnuts. What effect do you think luxury food such as this would have had on the morale of soldiers whose usual food was unappealing and often in short supply?

Salvation Army making Doughnuts under bombardment of German Guns, Front Line - France.

The exception to the rule that women did not fight on the front line was the 1st Russian Women's Battalion of Death—the only female fighting force in the war. Maria Bochkareva, who had gained the Tsar's permission to fight and was twice wounded, called for recruits at a time when Russia was going through revolution. About 2,000 women joined up. There were other isolated examples of women on the front line, such as Dorothy Lawrence, a British woman who spent some time in the trenches disguised as a male soldier before being discovered.

Maria Bochkareva is shown in this photograph with other female soldiers. Part of the campaign behind the recruitment of female soldiers was to shame male soldiers who had deserted the Russian army and discourage others from doing so.

Taking Over Tasks

Later in the war, governments needed to send every man they could to serve on the front line. Women took over many administrative roles. In Britain, the Women's Army Auxiliary Corps (WAAC) was set up in 1917. Members wore **khaki** uniforms and were organized in similar ranks to the regular army. The WAACs took on many support roles, including cooking, managing stores, driving trucks, and tending cemeteries. They were highly valued by the troops, not least because the food they prepared was said to be better than that of regular army cooks.

CHAPTER 4

HARDSHIP AT HOME

Most adults were involved in the war—either fighting or supporting the efforts to win it. Even if they were not directly involved, the war changed the lives of families far from the front line.

A War on Every Front

World War I was one of the first "total wars." The countries involved had to use everything at their disposal, including industry, farming, and even the media, to secure victory. These economic tools were operated by civilians, so ordinary people found themselves in the firing line. Aircraft and other new weapons could reach farther than ever before.

Howard Chandler Christy created this poster. The woman represents the United States and the words encourage people to sign up to fight or buy bonds. The money that people paid to buy bonds went toward paying for the war.

Not a High-Tech World

Home life before the war was very different from modern life. Most of the technology we take for granted today either did not exist or was in its early stages. Automobiles had been around for a few years, but they were only just becoming affordable for ordinary people. The first airplanes flew just a few years before war broke out. The war was a time of changing technology and big changes in society.

Controlling People's Lives

In order to organize and supply the military forces of the war, governments got more involved in people's lives than ever before. Industries such as railroads had to be controlled by governments to make sure they could transport troops effectively. Governments also tried to control what people heard and wrote about the war. Almost every area of life was more closely controlled than before the conflict.

PRIMARY SOURCE

A Fight Worth Fighting?

News from the front line was heavily controlled, and governments used persuasive words and images to make families believe that the war was a worthwhile fight. This poster has the words "Daddy, what did YOU do in the Great War?" What effect do you think they had on men who read them? Do you think they would have persuaded men to join the fight?

Daddy, what did YOU do in the Great War?

Families in Fear

Most armies did not set out to target civilians during the war, but powerful new weapons threatened families as never before. Families who lived in the conflict zones suffered most, as their homes were destroyed, and they were forced to flee. However, cities far from the front line were endangered by air attacks during the war.

Refugees on the Run

Belgium was invaded by Germany at the start of the war. Britain and France spread many stories about crimes committed by German troops against the Belgians. Only some of these were true, but hundreds of thousands of Belgians did flee from the invaders. Around 250,000 of them took refuge in Britain. Other Belgians were forced to work in Germany. People in Poland and Serbia also suffered terribly.

A Terrible Act

One of the greatest crimes against civilians in World War I took place in Turkey. Turkey's Armenian people were **persecuted** by their rulers and chose to side with Russian forces against them. Turkey's response was the murder of more than 1 million men, women, and children from the Armenian community.

Attacks in the Air

Air attacks on civilians were a new and frightening feature of the war. Germany used **zeppelins** to attack cities such as Paris and London. As aircraft technology developed, fighters could bring down the slow-moving airships. Later in the war, both sides used bomber aircraft, mainly for bombing industrial and military targets.

Attacks at Sea

Merchant and passenger ships also faced attack by submarines. The most infamous was the sinking of the RMS *Lusitania* in May 1915. The outraged public in Britain and the United States believed this was unprovoked, but it was later discovered that the British liner had been carrying munitions for the Allies, just as Germany had claimed after the attack.

The sinking of the *Lusitania* caused outrage among people on both sides of the Atlantic Ocean, and strengthened the resolve of the Allies to defeat Germany.

A Fight for Food

The war put a great strain on food supplies in all the countries of Europe. This was partly because a lack of men and horses on the farms meant that crops were not planted and harvested efficiently. The fighting made some farmland unavailable, and blockades enforced by warships and submarines prevented food arriving from overseas.

President Woodrow Wilson was the 28th president of the United States. Part of his US Food Administration campaign was to encourage meatless, sweetless, wheatless, and porkless days each week.

Families Go Hungry

Women and children lining up for food became a common sight in many European cities. Germany and Austria-Hungary introduced **rationing** early in the war to make sure there was enough to go around. By the end of the war, thousands of people were starving in Central Europe. This was also the case in Russia, where the war stopped food from the south reaching the northern cities. Eventually, food shortages led to the revolution against the country's rulers in 1917.

Not So Desperate

Britain and France fared better due to good organization and to some imports getting through, despite the threat of submarine attack. The WLA and other schemes tried to grow as much as possible and helped produce more food. But they still had to introduce rationing later in the war.

Saving Supplies

When the United States entered the war, President Woodrow Wilson set up the US Food Administration. Its job was to make sure there was enough food for American and Allied soldiers—and for the people of the United States and her allies. They believed this could be achieved by encouraging people to eat less and not waste food. A campaign of posters and information reduced food consumption by 18 million tons (16.3 million tonnes), which could then be sent overseas.

War in the Kitchen

This poster from World War I shows a woman cooking with cornmeal, oats, and barley, and shows the words "she is doing her part to help win the war." This was part of the campaign to encourage people to cook and eat with care to reduce waste. What effect do you think the words "doing her part" may have had on women who saw the poster?

she is doing her part to help win the war

Rationing Food

As a result of the US Food Administration campaign, some parts of the United States did suffer from food shortages. To try and ensure fairness across the country, rationing began in 1918. Ration cards were issued to all Americans, and butchers and grocers were not allowed to give more food than the cards authorized.

Posters such as this one encouraged people to believe that the rationing of food was as important to the war effort as the supply of ammunition.

Food is Ammunition— Don't waste it.

UNITED STATES FOOD ADMINISTRATION

31

War Children

Children in wartime had to cope with shortages and the threat of attack, just as their parents did. Millions of boys and girls were forced to say goodbye to fathers and brothers who left to serve on the front line. They did not know if their loved ones would return, and many would lose a family member in the fighting. In the United States, more than 360,000 children had to grow up without fathers after theirs were killed in the war.

Lessons in War

Children would not have heard much about the conditions in the trenches, or what was really happening in the war, although many would have known of soldiers who had been killed or wounded. Some textbooks from the time even show that the war was used as an example for math problems. Before 1917, the United States was neutral, and many families would have been supporting Germany. Once the United States had declared war, schools encouraged children to be **patriotic** and support US troops.

Youth Workers

Because their mothers were often working, older children were expected to spend more time looking after their younger brothers and sisters. Many teenagers were also working for the war. Children usually left school in their early teens and took jobs, including work in the munitions factories. Youth organizations such as the Boy Scouts and Girl Scouts raised money for the war.

Children's Changed Lives

War was a lesson that children could not escape. It became part of their learning at school, where they would learn patriotic songs and hear about important victories.

This photograph shows children at play during the time of World War I. Although they are dressed for fun, their experience of childhood would have been very different to that of children who had never lived through war.

This photograph shows German boys being trained for war. In Germany, boys as young as 17 years old were sent to the front line.

PRIMARY SOURCE

Taking Shelter

From 1915 to 1918, Britain suffered approximately 50 bombing raids that resulted in about 550 deaths and 1,350 injuries. This photograph shows British nannies with the children they cared for hiding in a bomb shelter during World War I. What do you think it must have been like for both the nannies and the children? What emotions do you think they may have experienced?

The Information War

Most information about the war came from newspapers and other printed information, such as posters. There were no TV or radio broadcasts, although some films of the war were shown in movie theaters. Public information was strictly controlled, and governments used **propaganda** to influence what people thought about the war. Letters home from the front line were also read—and **censored** if they revealed too much about what was happening in the trenches.

Persuading People

US President Woodrow Wilson set up the Committee of Public Information to organize publicity and propaganda for the US war effort, headed by George Creel. Americans did not all support the war, and Creel used new techniques to convince people. He employed "four-minute men" to make short speeches in movie theaters to persuade people to buy war bonds. The United States also passed laws to prevent people openly criticizing the war.

This famous poster encouraged American men to join the US army and fight for their country.

Hiding the Truth

Governments carefully controlled news from the front line, to make sure people back home were not fully aware of the horrors of the war. They were concerned that if families realized what their sons, husbands, and brothers were experiencing, the support for the war would greatly weaken.

This story from a French hospital was published in a British newspaper in 1914. It is titled "Cheerful Wounded."

It was Sunday and therefore visiting day in the hospital. There were little groups around the bedsides of the French wounded—mothers, wives, and children. What a light-hearted courage the wounded have! As I entered one ward, there was a sound of singing. It came from the bed of the most cruelly injured man there.

THE GREATEST SPECTACLE
THE WORLD HAS EVER SEEN
FOR THE GREATEST NEED
THE WORLD HAS EVER KNOWN

BRITISH TANK "BRITANNIA" IN ACTION

GRAND
CENTRAL
PALACE **HERO LAND** NOV. 24TH TO DEC. 12TH ADMISSION 50¢

FIRST IN FRANCE

U.S. MARINE

Propaganda on both sides presented the war as a fight between good and evil. Organizations such as Britain's War Propaganda Bureau produced books, films, and posters supporting the war.

WITNESS TO WAR

Despite the attempts to control people's minds on both sides of the war, in the later stages of the war, the mood was distinctly changing in Germany. Heinrich Beutow was a German schoolboy in 1917. His account records what people around him were saying about the war at that time.

What conditions within the country may Heinrich have been talking about?

"There was a strong sense of people saying 'This war is lasting too long.' Some people became quite outspoken. The feeling was that the war was lasting too long and that Germany didn't have much chance of winning it, because the conditions within the country were getting so very difficult."

CHAPTER 5

WINNERS AND LOSERS

When the war began in 1914, many people in Europe felt optimistic. They believed the fighting would last only a few months. Very few people thought the war would last for more than four years and claim millions of lives. By the start of 1918, governments and military leaders were no longer predicting or planning a quick end to the war. Yet, in November 1918, the war ended. How did this happen?

Russia Revolts

Russia's people suffered more than most from the shortages of the war, and their soldiers were very poorly equipped. In early March 1917, frustrations boiled over in a revolution that overthrew the Tsar. In November 1917, the **communist** Bolsheviks took power. They soon started to agree a peace treaty with Germany, so they could concentrate on fighting a civil war against their enemies at home. Germany could now focus on the Western Front, and things looked bleak for the Allies.

This is a photograph of Russian soldiers in Petrograd (St Petersburg) in 1917, happy with the news that their part in the war was over.

This photograph shows German soldiers marching through France during a push to overcome the Allied troops in the spring of 1918.

Sick of War

By 1917, the two sides on the Western Front had been at a standstill for three years. Attacking the enemy's trenches directly led to very high **casualties** for the attackers. Shell explosions and rain churned up the landscape in which the armies fought. Governments also found it harder to hide the horrors of the fighting from the families back home. The catastrophic battles at Verdun and the Somme in 1916 had caused devastating loss of life on both sides. People were sick of war and, in 1917, there was a wave of **mutinies** in the French army, accompanied by strikes in French cities. In early 1918, there were also strikes and riots in Germany and Austria-Hungary.

Winning the War

The Germans seemed to have a small advantage at the beginning of 1918, but in the long-term the balance of power would change decisively, and the Germans knew it. This was partly a result of US troops joining the fight but was also due to the organization and efforts of men, women, and children on the **home front**. When the United States joined the Allies they boosted the war effort with both supplies and money. Although the US had been an important supplier to the Allies in the early years of the war, they now began to focus their industry on military production. And when more troops were needed, they mobilized support with the use of conscription (draft).

Turning the Tide

When US troops arrived in France in spring 1918, the armies that had been fighting since 1914 were running out of soldiers. Germany and Austria-Hungary knew that 1918 was their last chance to win the war, and they launched a desperate offensive in March 1918. For several weeks they pushed French and British forces back deep into France. However, in July of that year, the Western Allies—now boosted by half a million US soldiers—began to fight back. The Germans were exhausted and had few reserves to call on. Meanwhile, the Allies were going from strength to strength. By November, the number of US troops on the Western Front had risen to around 2 million.

Home-Front Wins

The Allies were also winning the war on the home front. Their factories were producing more tanks, aircraft, and shells. Families might have complained about rationing in Britain and France, but this ensured that there was enough food to go around. In Germany, the government was totally focused on supplying the soldiers, and their families often faced starvation.

PRIMARY SOURCE

Turning Points

This photograph shows US troops joining the fight on the Western Front. What effect do you think the sudden increase in number of US soldiers had on the morale of both the Allies and the Germans?

US troops faced fierce fighting in a desolate landscape, such as the destroyed woodland shown here, when they entered the war.

WITNESS TO WAR

Fighting was very fierce right up to the Armistice in November 1918. This account of the fighting was written by a US Artillery soldier, Private McGuire.

"The situation at the Front was getting worse all the time. Because of the mud we couldn't sleep. Our kitchens were getting left behind, so we were hungry. It was a case of do or die now. ... Then we heard there was to be an armistice, so we were to fire off all our shells; otherwise we were going to have to take them back home."

What do you think it must have been like to fight in these conditions, and what would have motivated soldiers to continue?

What do you think McGuire meant by "do or die"?

An armistice is an agreement by both sides to stop fighting.

After fighting in such terrible conditions, how do you think soldiers like Private McGuire felt on hearing that the war was coming to an end?

CHAPTER 6

LIFE AFTER THE WAR

When World War I finally ended, Europe was in chaos. Some countries, such as Russia and Germany, were shaken by revolution. Others had to adjust to the devastating human and financial cost of the war.

A Terrible Toll

In the months following the war, people began to count the cost. Around 10 million soldiers had died in the war, leaving families without fathers, sons, and brothers. The death toll of civilians from enemy attack, starvation, and other crimes such as the Armenian massacres, was probably just as great. Many millions of soldiers were wounded in the war, having to continue life without legs and arms, or with mental scars from their experiences of war. Many of them were totally changed from the people who had gone to war in 1914.

Flu Becomes the Front Line

Immediately after the war, a disease known as Spanish Flu swept across the world, carried by soldiers returning from Europe. It claimed more lives than the war itself, especially in the United States, where the flu killed 550,000 people, in addition to the 50,000 Americans who died in battle.

This photograph shows a hospital in Kansas during the Spanish Flu outbreak in 1918.

British troops marched through Lille in France to a joyful welcome from the French when they liberated the city that had been occupied by German soldiers for four years.

What Was Gained?

In those countries that did not immediately erupt in revolution, political leaders vowed to create a new world from the disaster of World War I. In Britain, all adult men were allowed to vote in elections for the first time. Women had campaigned for the vote before the war. After the war, they finally achieved their goal in many countries, including Great Britain (where women over 30 were trusted with the vote), the United States, Canada, Germany, and elsewhere.

These French women are emerging from the cellar in which they hid during fighting in their town.

During the Great Depression (see opposite), soup kitchens like this one opened to feed hundreds of hungry people who found themselves in extreme poverty.

The Legacy of War

Having to live without loved ones was just one of the ways in which the world changed for many families after 1918. The years after the war were difficult times, with many of those who had fought in the war facing economic problems and unemployment. There were, however, some benefits, such as medical advances made during the war.

No Going Back

Soldiers returning from the war wanted to go straight back to their old jobs, but things were not always so simple. Industries such as shipbuilding and steelmaking had been boosted by the demand during wartime. This did not continue after the war, and there was widespread unemployment—even in the nations that had been victorious. The United States had been strengthened by the war's impact on its European rivals, but it was not able to escape economic problems altogether.

Not a Fair Fight

During the war, women had proven that they could handle many jobs and responsibilities that had been closed to them before. Although some of these gains were lasting, many women found themselves out of a job when male workers returned from the war.

Hopes for the Future

The families who emerged from the war hoped that their children would never have to experience anything like it. Many people also wanted to punish Germany for starting the war. At the post-war peace conference, the victorious countries demanded crippling compensation payments from Germany and redrew the map of Europe, reducing Germany's territory.

Trouble to Come

Unfortunately, the treatment of Germany after World War I prepared the ground for a strong leader to emerge, promising he would make Germany great again. Just 20 years later, Adolf Hitler would plunge the planet into a second world war, more terrible than the first.

Some people believe that Hitler may never have risen to power if Germany had not been so harshly treated after World War I.

Remembering the War

The terrible sacrifices of those who lived through World War I are remembered to this day, and their accounts as witnesses to history will shine a light forever on the horror of war.

A Long Reach

The financial issues caused by World War I would have far-reaching effects, and were partly responsible for a terrible economic downturn that took place at the end of the 1920s. It was called the Great Depression, and during this time of economic turmoil many people in Europe and the United States lost their jobs and experienced great poverty. In Germany, the extreme hardship was one of the factors for the popularity of Adolf Hitler, who promised to solve the country's economic issues. But worse was to come when Hitler took his country into the devastating World War II.

A TIMELINE FOR WAR

This timeline charts the key events of World War I.

1914

June 28: The assassination of Archduke Franz Ferdinand, heir to the throne of Austria-Hungary, takes place. Austria-Hungary blames Serbia and threatens military action.

July 28–August 4: Major powers of Europe declare war on each other. Germany and Austria-Hungary take up arms against France, Great Britain, Russia, and Belgium.

Early September: The first Battle of the Marne, near Paris, halts the German invasion of France, and trench warfare begins on the Western Front.

October 29: The Ottoman Empire (modern Turkey) enters the war on the same side as Germany and Austria-Hungary.

1915

January 19: The first zeppelin raid on Britain takes place.

April: Allied forces land at Gallipoli in the Dardanelles, northwestern Turkey. They are evacuated in January 1916 after heavy casualties.

May 7: RMS *Lusitania* is sunk by a torpedo from a German submarine with the loss of 1,198 lives.

May 23: Italy joins the war on the side of Britain, France, and Russia.

September: A major Allied attack is launched at Loos, on the Western Front.

1916

February 21: The Battle of Verdun begins in France—one of the bloodiest battles of the war.

May 31: In the North Sea, the Battle of Jutland begins between British and German navies.

July 1: The start of the Battle of the Somme on the Western Front. Almost 60,000 British troops are killed or wounded on the first day.

1917

February 1: Germany declares unrestricted submarine warfare, threatening to sink without warning any ships supplying the Allies, even if they are from the neutral United States.

March 8: The beginning of the Russian Revolution, which deposes Tsar Nicholas II and throws Russia's war effort into chaos.

April: A wave of mutinies and strikes by French soldiers and workers protesting against the war takes place.

April 6: The United States declares war on Germany.

May 18: The Selective Services Act introduces conscription (draft) in the United States.

July 31: The Battle of Passchendaele, near Ypres, Belgium, begins.

December 9: Allied forces in the Middle East capture Jerusalem.

1918

March 3: Russia's new government agrees peace with Germany in the Treaty of Brest-Litovsk, giving up large areas of territory in Eastern Europe and freeing up German forces to concentrate on the Western Front.

March 21: Germany launches a major attack on the Western Front, forcing Allied forces to retreat.

May: First American forces in action on the Western Front, led by General John Pershing. By this time, around 500,000 American troops are stationed in France.

July: British, French, and US armies begin major offensives (attacks) on the Western Front.

September: Allied forces reach Germany's defensive Hindenburg Line. Within a few weeks, Germany seeks to end the war.

November 11: An armistice is agreed to end fighting between Germany and the Allies. Austria-Hungary had already signed an armistice a few days earlier.

GLOSSARY

ammunition material fired from a weapon, such as bullets or shells

artillery large guns used for long-distance fighting

assassination the killing of someone important, usually for political reasons

blockade when a place has been sealed off to prevent supplies, such as food, passing through

casualties people who are hurt or killed

censored restricted access to information, such as by controlling what newspapers print

colonies lands ruled by the government of another country

communist a person or group who believes in creating an equal society through government control of property and many other areas of life

conscripted forced to serve in the military

Eastern Front in World War I, the border between land controlled by Germany and Austria-Hungary and that controlled by Russia

evacuation moving people away from a dangerous location

home front people who stay in a country and work while their soldiers are fighting abroad

khaki brown color used in some military uniforms

labor unions organizations of workers formed to campaign for rights from their employers

mobilize to prepare armies for war

munitions weapons, ammunition, and other supplies needed in war

mutinies when groups of people rise up, refuse orders, and try to take control

nationalists people from a political group that strongly campaign for national independence

neutral not favoring one side or the other

Ottoman Empire lands controlled from what is now Turkey, which included large areas of the Middle East in 1914

patriotic strongly supporting your home country

persecuted being targeted or discriminated against

propaganda information designed by a government or organization to promote a particular message

rationing restricting how much food and other items people can buy to ensure there is enough for everyone

respite a break or relief from something difficult

shells explosives fired from an artillery gun

Western Front in World War I, the border between land controlled by Germany and the Western Allies, where heavy fighting took place

zeppelins giant gas-filled airships, used by the Germans as bombers in World War I

FIND OUT MORE

Books

Captivating History. *American History for Kids: A Captivating Guide to Major Events in US History* (History for Children). Captivating History, 2023.

DK. *World War I* (DK Eyewitness). DK Children, 2023.

Mack, Louise, and various. *World War I Memoirs: First-Hand Recollections of the Battles, Dramas and Tragedies of 'The War to End All Wars'*. Arcturus, 2021.

Websites

Find out more about World War I at:
kids.britannica.com/kids/article/World-War-I/353933

The Imperial War Museum in London, England, has an enormous collection of resources about World War I:
www.iwm.org.uk

Visit the United States' National World War I Museum in Kansas City, MO:
www.theworldwar.org

Publisher's note to educators and parents:
All the websites featured above have been carefully reviewed to ensure that they are suitable for students. However, many websites change often, and we cannot guarantee that a site's future contents will continue to meet our high standards of educational value. Please be advised that students should be closely monitored whenever they access the Internet.

INDEX

About the Author

Kelly Roberts has written many history books for young people. In researching the eyewitness accounts in this book, she has learned more about the human experience of war and the devastation it caused for those who witnessed it.